KEYS

Their history and collection

ERIC MONK

Shire Publications Ltd

ACKNOWLEDGEMENTS

The author and publishers gratefully acknowledge the help of Messrs Josiah Parkes and Sons Ltd in their provision of photographs of exhibits in the Company Museum at Willenhall, West Midlands. Other illustrations are acknowledged as follows: page 21, Victoria and Albert Museum (Crown copyright); page 29, Science Museum. Thanks are also due to David Guy and Michael Glasson of the Walsall Library and Museum Service.

Line drawings by Eric Monk.

Published in 1999 by Shire Publications Ltd, Cromwell House, Church Street, Princes Risborough, Buckinghamshire HP27 9AA, UK. Website: www.shirebooks.co.uk Copyright © 1974 and 1999 by Eric Monk. First published 1974; reprinted 1979, 1983, 1987; reprinted with amendments 1994; second edition 1999. ISBN 0 7478 0422 2.

British Library Cataloguing in Publication Data: Monk, Eric. Keys: their history and collection 1. Locks and keys – Collectors and collecting I. Title 683.3'2 ISBN 0 7478 0422 2.

Printed in Great Britain by CIT Printing Services Ltd, Press Buildings, Merlins Bridge, Haverfordwest, Pembrokeshire SA61 1XF.

Victorian and Edwardian small keys.

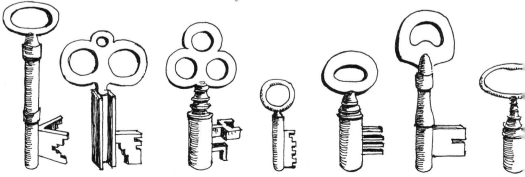

Contents

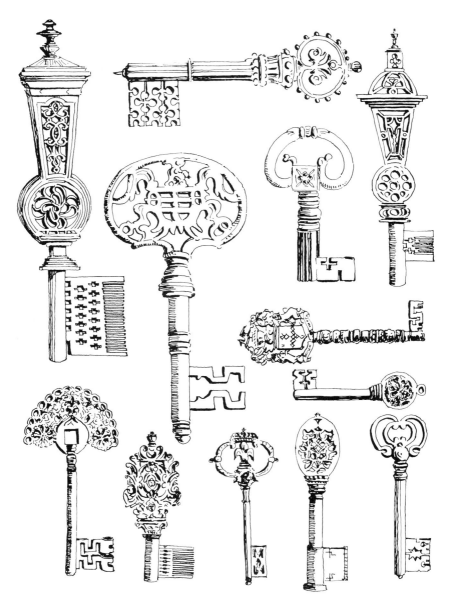

'Masterpiece' keys of the sixteenth and seventeenth centuries.

From latch to lock and key

The collecting of keys has gained popularity in recent years and this work is offered as a simple guide to the bewildering variety of types that may be found. Obviously, an understanding of the basic forms of locks must be gained, but this book is not intended as a technical treatise on the trade of the locksmith but as an aid to key identification. Whilst mention must be made of the incredible skill and artistry of the sixteenth-century keysmiths, and a few examples of what may be regarded as the 'Crown Jewels' of the key world are shown, priority is given to the sorts of keys that can be acquired by any collector, today.

Security is what the lock and key are all about, and since the very earliest times, when primitive man rolled a boulder against the mouth of his cave to keep out unfriendly neighbours or marauding animals, this need has been strongly felt. When he graduated from cave to hut and then discovered the luxury of a door, some early inventor proceeded to design a device to maintain his security. This device undoubtedly consisted of a stout wooden shaft which either slid between staples to seat into a slot in the jamb of the door, or was pivoted at one end and dropped into a hook at the other. The first type with its sliding 'bolt' developed along the ages into the modern lock, whilst the latter form of latch has not evolved, generally speaking, beyond the garden-gate type of fitting we know today.

Although these crude methods were effective against intruders when the hut was occupied, it was clearly not possible to seal the dwelling from the outside and thereby safeguard the contents during the owner's absence. The form of the first 'lock' to achieve this purpose can only be guesswork, as the only sources of information with references to locks are old myths and tales from China and the near East, while some mention of them may also be found in the Bible and in Homer.

The first lock to be found which was unquestionably of very great age was the wooden lock discovered on the site of the great palace of Sargon at Khorsabad, twenty miles north of Nineveh. A similar design was also drawn on the frescoes of the Temple of Karnak on the Nile. These findings and other clues prove that this type of lock is at the least 4,000 years old, but a strange fact is that locks of a similar pattern, based on the same mechanical principle, have been found in such diverse and remote areas as Scotland, Japan, Norway and America. More intriguing perhaps is the fact that such locks were still made until very recent times; an example of such a lock, purchased in 1935 by a director of Josiah Parkes (a firm dealing in locks and hardware), whilst in Zanzibar, is now displayed in the Company's museum at Willenhall. This lock is constructed exactly as the earliest Egyptian models and is of wood inlaid with bone decorations.

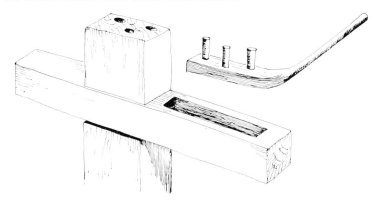

An Egyptian lock, at least four thousand years old.

The early Egyptian lock was fitted to the outside of the door and without resorting to sheer brute force it could not be operated without the correct 'key'. The horizontally sliding bolt contained several holes into which corresponding pins dropped when in the locked position. The pegs on the true key for the particular lock raised the pins, thus freeing the bolt, the handle of the key also serving as a lever to slide the bolt clear of its socket. The lock could also be secured from the inside, but this involved cutting a large hole in the door through which the arm could be placed and the key manipulated.

6

A lock made of wood with bone inlay. Constructed on the same principles as the earliest known Egyptian locks, it was bought in Zanzibar around 1935.

It has been suggested that this form of lock is one that would occur 'naturally' to anybody who set their mind to solving the problem of fixing and then releasing a sliding bolt. But this theory can hardly be reconciled with the fact that the principle lay forgotten for 4,000 years while locksmiths preoccupied themselves with the most tortuous and elaborate variations on an inferior basis.

The original wooden designs of the Egyptians were cumbersome but were followed by brass and iron locks which were often inlaid with other materials, including pearl. As the skill of these lockmakers increased so their fame spread and their work was required in far-off places — a possible explanation of the widespread occurrence of this form of security. However, as has

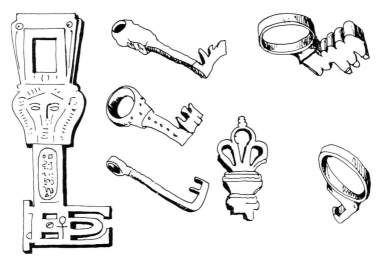

The sarcophagi key of King Ptolemis of Egypt, 300 B.C. (left), and Roman bronze finger-ring keys.

been said, the principle fell into disuse and the next type of lock which bears a relationship to the form that we know today was that used by the Greeks. They developed a system which for the first time incorporated a lockable bolt on the inside of the door: a hole some way above the bolt accommodated a long curved wooden key which was very much like a modern sickle both in shape and size. This key looped round, engaged the bolt, and on being turned actuated the bolt in basically the same manner as in modern locks. Unlike the convenience of the tiny slips of metal we carry today, however, the Greek keys were enormous and a wealthy owner would employ a slave to carry a bunch of them, crooked over his shoulder — Grecian status symbols.

As in so much work connected with building, it was not until the Romans came to the fore that locks and keys attained a fuller development. The best features of both Greek and Egyptian locks were used and the falling pins or 'tumblers' were cut in round, square, triangular and other more intricate geometric patterns. The keys for these were equally intricate and in many cases were small enough to form finger rings and served a double purpose as signets. Being made largely of bronze, which is a corrosion resistant metal, many have survived until today, unlike the Roman locks which, constructed of iron, have not come down to us in a complete form. Although attempts have been made to reconstruct replicas of Roman locks from the few parts that have been discovered, these are mainly conjectural, but suffice it to say that, obviously, a high degree of competence was reached in lock and key progress at this time.

A favourite device of the time in the safeguarding of possessions was the padlock, of which the Romans made wide use, as did other Mediterranean peoples and also Eastern races, particularly the Chinese. These were often made of brass and the practice of forming the cases in the shape of animals was very common.

The advanced skill of the locksmiths was illustrated strongly when excavations at Pompeii revealed a house which had been buried in the Vesuvius eruption of A.D. 64, apparently the home of a locksmith, for many examples of lock parts, padlocks and keys were found. One key was beautifully inlaid with silver and yet another was clearly a 'skeleton' or 'master' key.

Later Roman locks utilised obstacles in the path of the key to 'ward off' the entrance of an incorrect key and in these we can see the first use of 'wards' in the form which persisted for more than a thousand years until the Egyptian lock principle was resurrected by Linus Yale in the last century.

The Romans withdrew from Britain in A.D. 410 and subsequent invasions of Angles, Saxons and Jutes destroyed much of their building work, the remainder being allowed to crumble into decay. Britain relapsed into a barbaric state and few records of the life or buildings of the early Anglo-Saxon period have come down to us. It was not until about A.D. 600 that the increasing conversion to

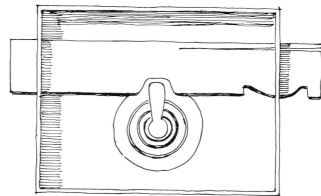

The interior of a back-spring warded lock without tumblers.

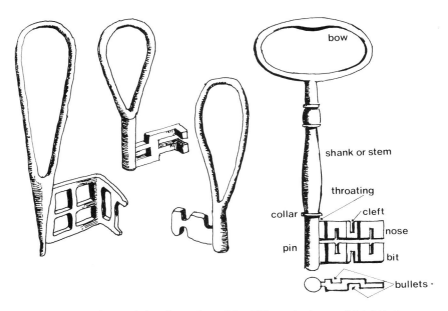

Three Norman keys of the eleventh and twelfth centuries, and (right) the parts of a key.

Christianity led to the building of churches in more permanent materials than those used for the huts of the villagers. The precise form of any locks and keys of this period must be largely guesswork, but since it is clear that skilled workers crossed the Channel to supervise more important building projects, Norman details were apparent long before the actual conquest of 1066.

Norman keys were, by modern standards, crudely forged and cut by blacksmiths and the large loop handle, later to be termed a 'bow', was very common, but oval and circular handles were also used. A wide range of sizes of keys and locks have been found, from those used for jewel cases to those for castle gates, and a study of the 'bits' or working end of the key shows that elaborate wards in the Roman manner were used.

10

Lock construction

Such locks were fitted to the 'grand' buildings — the castles and the churches — whilst humbler dwellings probably had simpler forms of security and it is doubtful whether the cottages of the peasants boasted more than wooden latches. Iron locks were expensive hand-made items, produced to the special orders of the Lord of the Manor, the Church or some other wealthy authority. It was not until the standardisation and mass production of the nineteenth century that locks and keys were available in sufficient quantities to become universal fittings.

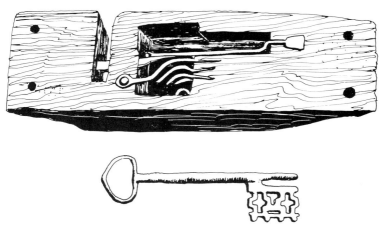

A fourteenth-century French lock and key in the Science Museum, London.

The basic type of lock construction of this period was much the same as the French lock and key on display in the Science Museum in London, where the wards are set into a roughly cut wooden block. In this particular lock the bolt has the same action as the latch type of fitting in that it is made to rise rather than slide. It is also of spring action so that the key is sprung to its original position when hand pressure is released — precisely like the modern Yale key. It can also be seen from the drawing that the amount of turn is some 90 degrees unlike the sliding bolt lock in which the key usually makes a full circle of 360 degrees before it can be withdrawn. Because of the absence of the spring, the sliding bolt is in locksmith's parlance termed a 'dead' bolt or the lock called a 'dead' lock.

Dead locks were also widely used by the Normans and numerous keys exist proving that quite intricate wards were cut although it can be seen that they were very open, the gaps or 'clefts' in the keys being several millimetres wide. Some of these early keys have solid stems or shanks while others are hollow and, for obvious reasons, are termed 'pipe' keys. It is true to say that the latter afford more security than the solid stem type since it was also necessary for the bore of the pipe to fit over a corresponding pin within the lock, in addition to passing the wards.

Whether the shank was solid or pipe, the basic construction of the lock could be the same in each case, the essential reason for the difference in the stem being that the solid key could operate the lock from both sides as in the door of a room, whilst the pipe key has a one-sided action such as would be needed for chests and furniture. Additional defence against the insertion of a false key was often obtained by the cutting of the keyhole into a more complex design than a mere slot and forming the bit of the key to suit it. In fact, this practice has been quite common, throughout the centuries until the present day, and in many cases the 'side ward', as it has sometimes been called, of the keyhole itself is the only security obtained from the lock and no internal wards are fitted. In the nineteenth century, when lock classifications were precise and numerous, such locks were in the category of 'plain'.

The loop bows of the early Norman keys were obviously at a disadvantage if the lock was to be fixed to a thick wooden door, which was required to be opened from both sides, and by the thirteenth century the most common types of bow were the simple round or oval combined with a straight, unadorned shank.

This then was the usual form of key at the time of Magna Carta and the Crusades and the sort of key, in miniature, that the gallant knight would carry with him to keep fresh the memory of his mistress at home in her castle in England. This was one key that has no place on modern man's key-ring — the key to the chastity belt, which was secured by a small padlock at his wife's waist. It is not known whether knights entertained any genuine faith in the efficiency of this lock, but in view of the proven fallibility of wards it is probably safe to say that the device was more symbolic than functional! Some authorities have, however, tended to deride this popular romantic aspect of the chastity belt and attribute its purpose to that of protection while the lady was travelling.

12

Warded locks and elaborate keys

When considering the development of architecture it is customary to allot certain terms to specific periods, for example Norman, Decorated, Perpendicular and Tudor. The development of locks and keys can be followed on similar lines although not in quite the same categories as architecture.

It has been seen that apart from early Roman work the first keys to resemble modern ones were those of the Normans, and this period of influence could therefore form our first classification. Typified by loop, round and oval bows, straight stems without collars and wide clefts to the bits, these keys bore an obvious hand-wrought, 'early craftsman' appearance.

As in architecture, where the massive arches and vaults of the Norman style gradually gave way to the lighter look of Early English, so locks and keys became more refined and ornamental. This, in turn, from around the year 1200, developed through styles taking their names from the windows of the times until the Tudor period of 1500–1560. Our subject cannot be so finely classified but the entire period from Norman to Tudor is often called Gothic, a word of disapproval applied by Renaissance architects to medieval architecture, and this period (otherwise known as the Middle Ages) could be used for the second category. This second period shows an increasing competence in the working of metal; far more use was made of ornament and more finely cut bits and, in particular, greater variety is found in the pattern of bows. The lozenge shape bow was popular in the fourteenth century and in the fifteenth century the 'Kidney' bow became the prevalent shape. It has been mentioned that Norman keys did not have a 'collar' or stop to prevent their being pushed too far through the lock and this device seems to have appeared in the fifteenth century.

The sixteenth century and the Elizabethan period saw the

A sixteenth-century steel lock, 17¼ by 13 inches, mounted in a wood frame to revolve in a pedestal. It was probably made for semi-flush fitting.

rebirth of classical learning — the Renaissance — and it is during this time that locks and keys reached the peak of the locksmith's skill and artistry. The final development of the lock began comparatively suddenly at the end of the eighteenth century when the stranglehold of the warded lock was broken and a flow of new ideas extended throughout the Industrial Revolution and the reign of Victoria.

As the skill of the locksmiths of the Middle Ages increased so did the skill of the thieves, indeed without the latter locks and keys would be unnecessary and there would be no story to tell! A perusal of the drawing showing the action of a key around a ward, and those (page 32) showing the ease with which the most elaborate and finest of cuts may be bypassed by a crudely bent wire, prove the fallibility of the system and this weakness was

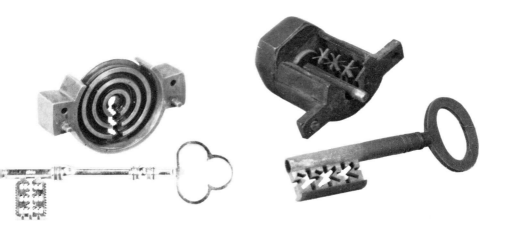

Above: two boxes of wards with keys.
Below: a Renaissance lock and key.

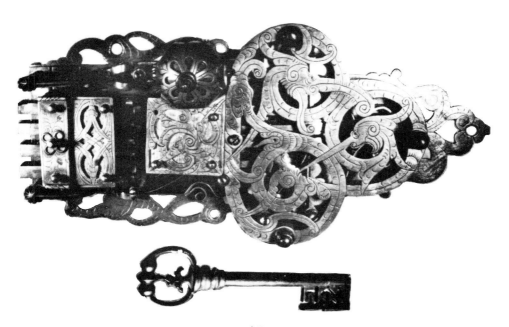

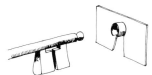

Simple form of ward.

acknowledged by the medieval craftsmen. One philosophy they adopted in attempts to overcome the problem was 'safety in numbers'. In their efforts to place the greatest possible deterrent before the thief, they fitted five locks in place of one or, trying to be ultra secure, even ten locks. Whilst this inevitably slowed down the process of lock picking, thieves were notoriously patient, so that the treasure chest of the Lord of the Manor was still highly vulnerable. In order to economise perhaps, for locks were still 'purpose-made to special order', to use twentieth-century parlance, a more ingenious locksmith would construct one lock which required several keys. In 1415 it is recorded that Isabelle of Bavaria commissioned the building of a lock which needed five keys to operate it. This was fitted to the doors of the chambers of the ladies-in-waiting in order to exclude unwelcome visitors (and gratings were fitted over the chimney openings!).

Henry II of France clearly did not welcome the inconvenience of five separate keys for one lock. The locksmith who executed a 'security system' for him put in a 'master key' scheme which is now common practice in hotels and similar buildings today. He had fitted to the door of his mistress's apartment no less than three locks, each having a different ward arrangement. Success at opening one lock with key or 'pick' would not be followed with an 'open sesame' at the other two, but the king's master key would work all three.

The most common form of multiplication, and the most fallacious, was that used on treasure-chests or coffers, in which the number of bolts to the lock was increased to twelve, twenty-four

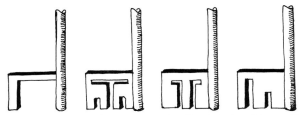

The 'skeleton' or 'master' key principle. The left-hand key will open all the other locks.

An inside view of a chest lid.

or even more. These were spaced around the perimeter of the lid of the chest, and at the centre of a veritable spider's web of arms, levers and pivots was situated the lock mechanism itself. Writing of such a chest in 1767 M. de Réaumur says it was 'known in Paris as the Strong German Coffer and nothing is wanting in these chests in the score of solidarity. They are made entirely of iron, or if of wood, they are banded both within and without with iron, and can be broken open only by very great violence. Their locks are almost as large as the top of the coffer and close with a great number of bolts. Notwithstanding the large size of these locks and all the apparatus with which they are provided, they correspond but ill with the solidity of the rest of the coffer.' The whole device appears to our eyes as something of a confidence trick — the seemingly impregnable construction may have impressed the gullible baron who had commissioned it, but it is hardly likely to have caused the medieval robber much difficulty. Having set his pick-lock to overcome the solitary group of wards in the customary manner, he must have derived considerable satisfaction and no little amusement from feeling all twenty-four bolts move simultaneously free under the turn of his hand.

17

The Armada chest.

After the 'safety in numbers' approach, it seems incredible that with the vastly increased proficiency of the craftsman, still no improvement on the basic action of the wards was effected. Instead, the deftness of the smiths was directed mainly at decoration, and locks and keys were adorned with scroll patterns and representations of animals, birds, lavish leaf designs and heraldic devices. The latter became quite popular, as many of the locksmiths' customers (or perhaps the word patrons might be

18

more appropriate) were of the nobility. In fact our present use of the term 'escutcheon plate' derives from those times when the escutcheon or coat-of-arms of the owner was formed into a small plate which either slid or pivoted over the keyhole of a lock to conceal it. This escutcheon was often constructed so that it was necessary to press a knob or a certain part of the lock's decoration in order to release it. The placing of false keyholes in the centres of doors and chests was also tried, locating the true keyhole behind an escutcheon in some other obscure spot.

One of the most famous locks of this type is built in the form of the front elevation of a house, with portico and windows and no obvious aperture for the insertion of a key at any point. It is essential to press a small hidden spring in order to spring open one of the windows revealing the knobs to the four bolts of the lock.

An etched jewel casket made in Nuremburg in the late sixteenth century. It is fastened by two spring bolts at front and two fixed dog bolts at back.

Having shot these bolts, it is not possible to move them again by any obvious manipulation. Instead, yet another secret spring must be found, which when pressed causes the centre doorway to open on hinges and at last the keyhole is seen.

The key to this lock is also unique: it is some six inches long and has in effect two shanks, the outer being of square section and chiselled into the shape of a lantern, and an inner stem revolving within the other end carrying a comparatively small bit. This bit consisted of seventeen fine clefts and twelve square holes in an area of some five-eighths of an inch. When it is considered that these cuts married up to the similarly formed wards within the lock, it is almost impossible to understand how such intricate and precise work could have been executed with (compared with twentieth-century technology) what must have been crude and rudimentary tools.

What is even more remarkable is that many of these locks, which have fortunately been preserved and may now be seen in museums and private collections, were made by apprentices who, in serving their ten years' apprenticeship in order to become journeymen, were called upon to make a special lock and key. Such locks are often termed 'masterpiece' locks and several years ago a lock of this type was carefully stripped down to its smallest part and each item scrupulously examined and analysed. The experts who carried out this inspection reached a verdict that some three thousand hours of time had been spent on this lock, which, on the basis of a modern forty hour week, represents about eighteen months' work!

The key also received its share of attention and the key-ring in particular became more decorative and flamboyant until its function as a ring was lost and a small ring was often added above the miniature sculpture in steel that occupied much of the shank. The cuts in the bits of keys and the corresponding wards over which they fitted were formed in the shapes that were in vogue at the time, crosses and fleur-de-lis, and anchor patterns were later popular.

In addition to a key, in some medieval locks it was also necessary to use a stiletto in order to spring the escutcheon plate, and the outer face of the lock being covered with a profusion of ornament rendered the location of a minute hole extremely difficult. The Beddington lock is one of the most famous in English history. This lock, which is some fourteen inches long, bears the coats-of-arms of both Henry VII and Henry VIII.

The Beddington lock was fixed to the bedroom doors of Henry VII and Henry VIII when they travelled through the country.

According to the records this security was very much respected by both kings who insisted on having it fixed to their bedroom doors when they travelled through the kingdom.

The constant striving for security and the thought and ingenuity applied to the subject of locks and keys are typified by the writings of the Marquis of Worcester who, in the early seventeenth century, put forward in his *Century of Inventions* some curious suggestions:

69. 'A way how a little triangle screwed key, not weighing a shilling, shall be capable and strong enough to bolt and unbolt, round about a great chest, an hundred bolts, through fifty staples, two in each, with a direct contrary motion; and as many more from both sides and ends; and, at the self same time, shall fasten it

to the place beyond a man's natural strength to take it away; and in one and the same turn both locketh and openeth it.'

70. 'A key with a rose-turning pipe and two roses pierced through endwise the bit thereof, with several handsomely contrived wards, which may likewise do the same effects.'

71. 'A key, perfectly square, with a screw turning within it, and more conceited than any of the rest, and no heavier than the triangle screwed key, and doth the same effects.'

72. 'An escutcheon, to be placed before any of these locks, with these properties: First, the owner though a woman, with her delicate hand vary the ways of causing to open the lock ten millions of times beyond the knowledge of the smith that made it, or of me that invented it.

'Second, if a stranger open it, it setteth an alarum a-going, which the stranger cannot stop from running out; and besides, though none shall be within hearing, yet it catcheth his hand as a trap doth a fox; and though far from maiming him, yet it leaveth such a mark behind it as will discover him if suspected; the escutcheon or lock plainly showing what money he hath taken out of the box to a farthing, and how many times opened since the owner had been at it.'

The trapping of the hand suggested by the Marquis was, in fact, similar to the lock that propelled a steel dart into the hand of anyone tampering with the mechanism that did not know its secret. It is reported that the locksmith injured himself in the process of demonstrating the action.

There were many variations on the sadistic theme of injuring or even killing the would-be thief and among these the most common was the additional lid that was fitted beneath the normal top of the large coffers already described. This inner tray contained a series of holes that appeared to be obvious finger grips; having successfully picked the lock and, as we have said, been amused at the ease with which all the multiple bolts moved back together, the smile on the luckless thief's face would be short-lived as he inserted his fingers in the 'lifting holes' of the inner lid. For a strong spring would immediately be released activating vicious steel jaws which latched on to his fingers almost to the point of amputation.

Another locksmith, who went the whole way, incorporated a pistol behind the lock which fired point blank at anyone who had not operated the secret safety catch before trying to open the

Iron chest locks

Above: a chest lock and key.

Left: a massive iron chest lock, with key (below).

lock. Yet another alternative was the sudden discharge of a blast of pepper into the face of the tamperer.

The idea of the alarum was not neglected and some locks incorporated the obvious device of a bell, although perhaps the types listed above were the most effective in this respect since the scream of agony caused by them would be more penetrating than the ringing of a bell. Alarms, hidden keyholes, maiming devices, multiple locks, multiple keys and multiple bolts: all these were tried with varying degrees of success, but another line of thought was the combination or puzzle lock. Possibly the best known of these, dating from the end of our Middle Period of lock making, was made by Johannes Wilkes of Birmingham. This is decorated in high relief with the figure of a man pointing with a stick at a dial surrounded by numbers and bearing the engraved verse:

'If I had ye gift of tongue
I would declare and do no wrong
who ye are yt com by stealth
to impare my Masters welth.'

The dial registered the number of times the lock had been opened, but it was necessary to lift the man's legs by pressing a secret button before the keyhole was revealed, and the catch could not be operated until his hat was raised.

Locks were also constructed on the pure combination principle, without keys, it being necessary to know the code word to which to set a series of lettered rings — a method still in use today.

As in so many articles which are utilitarian, it is the outstanding example which is preserved, the Rolls Royce rather than the Austin Seven, the silver casket rather than the wooden box. Similarly, in the field of locks and keys, it is relatively easy to study the supreme examples of the metal workers' art, most of which were not intended to fulfil a day-to-day function but were exhibition pieces or made as medieval status symbols to satisfy the whim or pride of the nobility. To find specimens of the equivalents of the Yale and Chubb keys of the twentieth century is not so easy, but such keys can occasionally be seen in the smaller local museums together with functional, and not merely decorative, locks.

The part of the lock most prized by collectors is the decorated face, which is usually termed the 'lock plate'. These items rarely change hands but they can realise many thousands of pounds each when they do. Early lock plates of the fourteenth century often used details from Gothic tracery and during the fifteenth century

A seventeenth-century German combined latch and night latch with three bevelled spring bolts, the upper one withdrawn by a handle or knob, the lower two by a key.

scriptural figures were popular. One famous plate represents the Last Judgement and contains thirty-five figures, while another one of this period bears the depiction of Christ and the twelve Apostles, each under a separate canopy. In the fifteenth century the Guild of Locksmiths was the most powerful body in France and the enormous popularity of locks is shown by records of that time. One report dated 1422 relates that the Hotel in Rue Bourdonnois was one of the curiosities of Paris, since it possessed as many locks as there are days in the year.

In the fifteenth century, England, disturbed by wars, lost her supremacy in the art of the blacksmith and the Flemings were capturing the trade of Europe. The French became renowned for ironwork chiselled from the solid, *'pris dans la masse'* as it was called. Later, the classic style was introduced by Francois I who paid a heavy price for locks at Fontainebleau and the *chateaux* at Madrid and Villers. The locksmith was Morisseau, who abandoned the solid chiselled work in favour of thin plates of iron decorated with arabesques in the Italian style — masks, dragons and cupids — but the handles remained carved from the mass and were often formed in the shape of human or animal heads.

When Louis XIII came to the throne in 1610 the older craft of chiselled iron was revived and Louis was a generous patron, being himself a highly competent locksmith. English locks of the same period did not achieve the high standard of the French, but later examples of the seventeenth century reached a greater degree of artistic skill with their pierced, chased and engraved brass plates over plain steel backs.

The whole Middle Age of the development of the lock and key is one of preoccupation with decoration, status symbols and the elevation of locksmithing to an art rather than a science. The period is linked with the romantic aspect of gallant knights, robber barons and treasure chests; massive locks and massive keys to dank dungeons. But perhaps the most famous and the most romantic of the tales that involves our subject is that of the key to Loch Leven Castle. In May 1568, when Mary Queen of Scots was held captive in Loch Leven, the boy, William Douglas, obtained the key, released the queen and her maid, rowed them across the lake and threw the key into the water to prevent pursuit. The key was later recovered and passed down from owner to owner until it was ultimately presented to Sir Walter Scott.

Keys of the sixteenth and seventeenth centuries, including (right) the key to Loch Leven Castle.

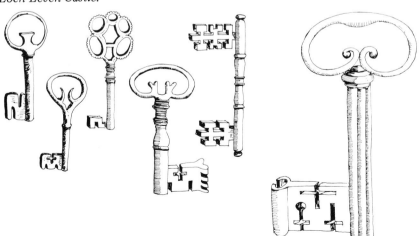

Innovations versus the lock-picker

The Middle Age of lockmaking — that is the period between the twelfth and eighteenth centuries — with its increasing decoration, but centred solely on the warded lock, ended during the reigns of the four Georges and Victoria.

Right down the ages, it is true to say that the literature of locks and keys has been extremely scanty despite the obvious popularity of the subject. The reason for this is not difficult to understand, for it has often been stated that the very security that the lock affords would be weakened by the publication of explanations of its workings. Unfortunately, thieves have always been as cunning as locksmiths and as long as the mental block of adherence to wards was maintained, no publication on the topic would have been of benefit to the intending lock-picker.

The French and Germans appear to have been somewhat less reticent about the matter and several works of the eighteenth century give a clear picture of the craft at that time. The best known of these, *L'Art du serrurier*, was published in 1767 by the Académie des Sciences and formed part of a portfolio of treatises on various crafts and manufactures. The French word *serrurerie* applies to most of the smith's work in dwelling houses and consequently this book contains articles on all aspects of metalwork and ironmongery to be found in a house — the windows and window catches, gates and railings, hinges and door handles.

The article on locks and keys, however, occupies one hundred pages, illustrated by twenty plates, ranging from the simplest types of lock without wards up to more complex forms, and what is significant, showing that the lever tumbler lock was known at that time. But it was not until 1778 that Mr Robert Barron became the first person to patent a lock that took the lever tumbler principle a step further and at long last broke the supremacy that the wards

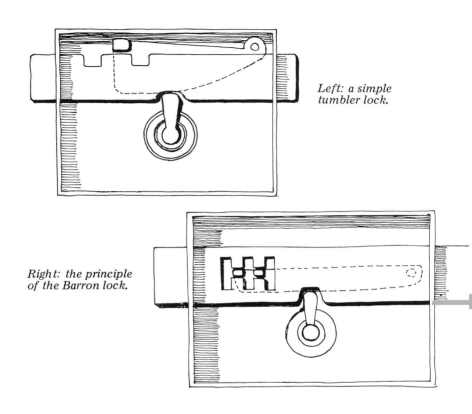

Left: a simple tumbler lock.

Right: the principle of the Barron lock.

had held. From the drawing of this type of lock it can be seen that in addition to raising the tumbler, it was now necessary to raise it by an exact amount. In fact, if the smith was precise in his work, a few thousandths of an inch either too high or too low in the action of the key would prevent the bolt from sliding, as the stump would not then clear the notches. Mr Barron made doubly sure of the efficiency of this device by introducing two tumblers which had to be lifted to different heights, so that it was essential for two stumps to be free of the notches to release the bolt. This

Opposite: an extract from 'L'Art du serrurier', a French book on locks and keys dated 1767.

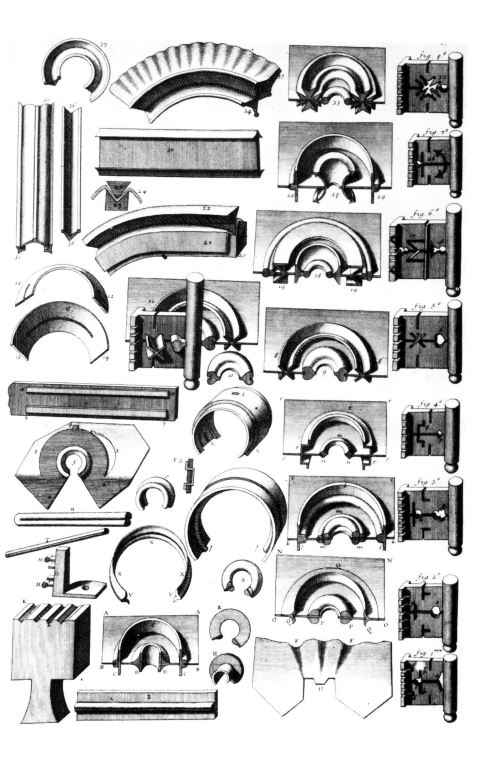

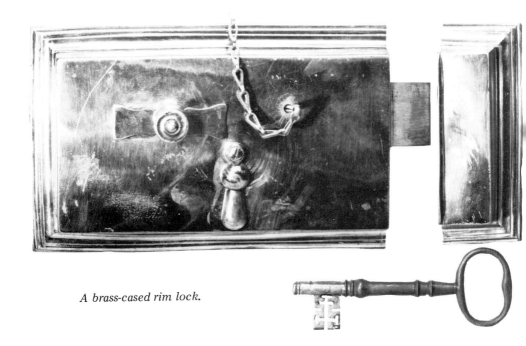

A brass-cased rim lock.

was an infinitely more difficult obstacle to overcome than the most complicated set of wards, but Mr Barron in his early locks did not omit the latter, just as early steam ships still carried a quota of sail.

The first patent for a lock appears to have been granted in the year 1774 and the next ones, dealing with lever locks, in 1790, when a Mr Rowntree invented a complicated tumbler lock utilising wheels and a Mr Bird, in the same year, brought out a modification to the Barron lock. Mr Bird merely took the ultimate step by eliminating wards completely and introducing four double-acting tumblers and, in fact, initiating the lever lock which is on sale today. The keys to lever locks may be instantly recognised by the steps in the nose to fit the differing heights of the levers.

There were some twelve patents issued during the next twenty-five years, but (with one outstanding exception, to be mentioned later) these had little influence on the ultimate design of locks as we have now come to know them.

30

In 1815 a further factor was added to the wards and the tumblers and that was the detention of a wrong key in the lock. The patent of Mitchell and Lawton in that year incorporated movable wards and a revolving curtain for closing the keyhole. The action was unusual in that the wards themselves moved and if a false key was inserted they were thrown out so as to prevent the key from being turned back or withdrawn. Since it was necessary to destroy the lock in order to remove the key, the lock does not appear to have come into regular use, but it does seem to have started the idea of detectors.

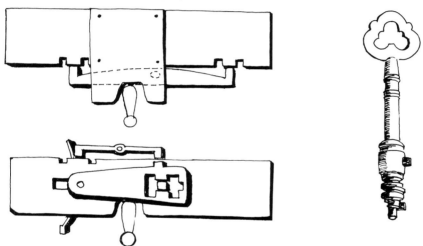

Left upper: the principle of Parsons' balance lever lock.
Left lower: the principle of the Chubb lock with detector.
Right: the key to Cotterills' 'Climax' detector lock, a nineteenth-century safe lock.

The first patent for a detector lock was made out to Ruxton in 1816 and the object was to provide information to the owner as to whether any attempt had been made to open the lock illegally. He also had a device which was of similar action to the previous one in that complete destruction was required to free the false key.

An improved form of detector was patented by Chubb in 1818 and there were subsequent patents in 1824, 1833, 1846 and 1847. The lock in its later form consisted of six double-acting tumblers or levers all of which had to be raised to a specific height as described before. The detector consisted of an additional lever

31

which was spring loaded and mounted above the six tumblers. If a false key raised any of the levers too high, the stump would be caught in the gate but also the lever would be held in the raised position by the detector. This would become immediately apparent on trying to open the lock with the true key, as it would fail to operate the bolt. Unlike its predecessors, however, it was not required to demolish the whole unit in order to free the key but the true key needed to be turned in the reverse direction, i.e. as if locking the door, and this had the effect of releasing the detector lever and any levers which had also been caught up.

From the mid-eighteenth century the concentration on decoration was reversed and locks and keys became very plain, some lock cases of this period are of smooth brass and the faces are completely free of any embellishment even that of screwholes. The keys of the time are, for better quality locks, well proportioned, the 'wire bows' are nicely formed, the stems turned in a typical Georgian fashion and the bits precisely cut.

The concentration now was on the improvement of the internal mechanics of the lock and the monopoly of the warded lock was broken. The facility with which the latter could be picked had long been accepted, but now it became a popular craze to challenge the new ideas and rewards were offered to anyone capable of opening certain locks and even lock-picking contests were held.

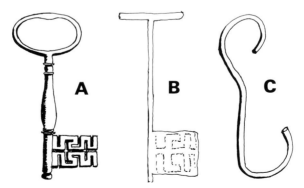

Lock-picking. A: the true key. B: instrument of flat metal covered with wax or soap to obtain 'print' or impression of wards. C: wire loop formed to bypass wards.

Lock-picking

In one case, a convict, held on board a prison ship at Portsmouth, maintained that he could pick one of the new Chubb locks with ease. This man was previously a lock-maker and had been working in London as such, until his fall from grace when he became notorious as a lock-picker. A Chubb lock was secured by the seals of Sir George Grey, the commissioner, and the convict was given not only a similar lock for examination but also all the necessary tools, blank keys and equipment he needed for the task. If he succeeded in picking the lock he was to receive a free pardon from the Government and £100 from Messrs Chubb. Having tried repeatedly for a period of three months and failed dismally, he announced that the Chubb lock was unpickable and he returned to prison.

Many inventions based on the principle of the lever tumbler were made in the early years of the nineteenth century, some of which gained awards from the Society of Arts, which interested itself in this sphere.

In 1784 a patent was granted to a type of lock which was completely different from anything previously produced and was a breakaway from all thinking on the subject. The invention was introduced by the publication of an essay, the full title of which was: 'A dissertation on the Construction of Locks. Containing, first, reasons and observations demonstrating all locks which depend upon fixed wards to be erroneous in principle, and defective in point of security. Secondly, a specification of a lock, constructed on a new and infallible principle, which possessing all the properties essential to security, will prevent the most ruinous consequencies of house robberies, and be a certain protection against thieves of all descriptions.'

The author and inventor was a Yorkshireman by the name of Joseph Bramah and he produced a lock that was, even by today's standards, a masterpiece of miniature engineering, as delicate and fascinating as a pocket watch, beautifully turned in brass, with a key as small as a modern 'Yale'.

Mr Bramah's reference to house robberies was well founded, since at the time of writing, in the middle of the reign of George III, house-breaking had risen to an alarming degree in London, and this was another factor in the increased impetus given to the whole question of security and lock design. After dealing in his essay with the weaknesses of warded locks Mr Bramah then turned his attention to the lever tumbler lock recently invented by Mr Barron of which he said: 'Greatly as the

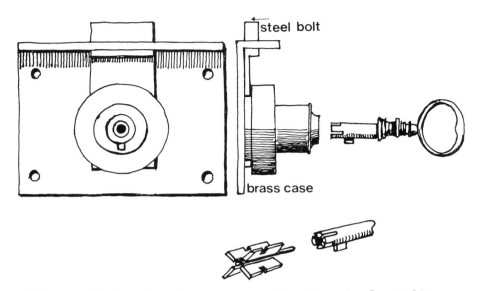

steel bolt

brass case

The Bramah lock and key, showing the principle of the action. Patented in 1784 this lock was at first considered unpickable.

art is indebted to the ingenuity of Mr Barron, he has not yet attained that point of excellence in the construction of his lock which is essential to perfect security.' He then went on to describe in detail how the lock could be picked and, to add insult to injury, how it could be improved.

Mr Bramah's own lock was based partly on the sliding principle of the ancient Egyptian lock and partly on the turning action which had been accepted as standard practice for the past thousand years. The first model which he illustrated in his dissertation was a flat lock using the same fundamental ideas that were incorporated in his subsequent cylindrical types.

It will be seen from the drawing that the security of the Bramah lock relied upon the sliders that were spaced radially around the pin over which the pipe key fitted. These sliders were set at differing heights which corresponded to the slots set round the end of the key stem. So the key was first pushed home against spring action, releasing the sliders from their notches, allowing the cylinder to turn and so slide the bolt. The small 'bit' on the key no longer served any security purpose as in a warded lock but merely served to engage a notch to turn the cylinder.

The Bramah lock was, because of its precise construction, very expensive, but they were made in considerable quantities and for some time were regarded as unpickable. Doubts crept in, however, following the ability of a London locksmith to open these locks with very fine steel forceps and indeed this skill was advertised in the newspapers; as the small keys were frequently lost, this ability saved many items of furniture from damage.

This was a serious blow to Joseph Bramah's self-styled infallibility, but one which was overcome by a member of his team of locksmiths who introduced false notches into the sliders, so that it was essential to move all the sliders together. The lock-picker's system had relied on being able to manipulate the sliders one at a time so that he was now defeated. The locksmith who devised this modification was a man called Russel and many of the Bramah locks produced bear the additional marking, 'W. Russel's security'.

Many words have been expended and many diagrams prepared to describe the action of the Bramah lock, but to the person who takes a delight in handling any piece of hand-made precision craftsmanship there is no substitute for the real thing. Beyond the brief description and basic sketch given here, suffice it to say that this is one lock that is not too difficult to acquire to accompany the key collection. Once the key has been lost, most antique dealers consign these little masterpieces to the rubbish heap; the author has obtained many examples and has yet to pay for one! Having stripped down a Bramah lock and re-assembled it correctly, the fact is forcibly brought home that for such an item to be made two hundred years ago, when locks of about eight by four inches with five inch long keys were common, was no mean feat.

Mr Russel restored public confidence in the Bramah lock and one of Bramah's padlocks (actually constructed by Maudslay, later to become one of our greatest engineers) rested in the shop window in Piccadilly together with the challenge that 200 guineas would be awarded to anyone who could pick it. It remained there for fifty years.

During the fifty years ending in the Great Exhibition of 1851, some seventy patents were granted and what has been called 'The Great Lock Controversy' raged. Battle was joined between rival lockmaking companies, between thief and locksmith and between nations. The Americans in particular were strongly interested in the matter of security and, if our television screens are to be believed, bank robbery seemed to be a favourite pastime in the earlier part of the nineteenth century.

Among the American locks of this time was one which was a development of the ancient Egyptian lock. The basis was a revolving plate pierced with a series of holes and on the lock case a matching set of spring-loaded pins. The action was similar to that of the Bramah lock in that it was necessary to turn the key and then apply pressure against the force of a spring to push the pins through the holes in the plate allowing it to turn and so actuate the bolt.

An early Yale lock combined the Bramah cylinder principle with that of the pins of the Egyptian lock and this was the forerunner of the most widely used lock in the world today. An early example contained no less than forty pins, so that the permutation of possible settings was astronomical.

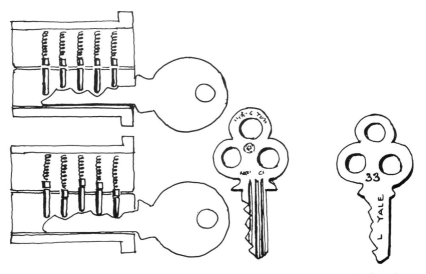

The Yale lock principle: the true key (upper left) aligns the gaps in the pin tumblers allowing the cylinder to turn, but a false key (lower left) misaligns the gaps and the cylinder remains locked.
Right: two old Yale keys.

Both American and English locksmiths were made aware that the thief rapidly found his way around each new development and as Bramah had been disconcerted so it became Chubb's turn to

A wall-safe door with locks and keys.

wear a red face. After the episode of the Portsmouth convict and following Bramah's criticism that the levers of the Chubb lock would probably not withstand continual wear, Chubb arranged a special demonstration. He connected the key, whilst in the lock, to a small engine which turned the key back and forth at high speed and this was allowed to turn 460,000 times. Examination of key and levers after the experiment revealed that wear was negligible.

Chubb's confidence was shaken, however, when it was found that it was possible to insert a lighted taper in the keyhole, 'smoke' the underside of the levers and obtain a 'print' on a skeleton key. By using a very small mirror, the interior of the lock and the smoked levers could be inspected, and eventually the lock opened without disturbing the detector. Chubb overcame this by incorporating a 'curtain' behind the keyhole to prevent just this sort of manipulation.

Now that locksmiths had defeated attempts to inspect the inside of a lock, through the keyhole, another factor remained and that was that the sight of the key or handling of it, even for a few seconds, by a potential thief still left the lock vulnerable. The first man to direct his efforts at meeting this difficulty was apparently a Mr Andrews of New Jersey. He approached the problem by making the tumblers of his lock variable and the bit of his key had separate segments which could also be varied to fit the alterations in the positions of the tumblers. At the same time, Mr Newell of the firm of Day and Newell of New York was engaged on a similar line of thought, but he utilised two sets of tumblers, primary and secondary, but the result was not entirely satisfactory and he even reverted to adding wards to boost the security and a curtain to cover the keyhole. Mr Newell's high hopes of success with the final model were dashed when an American machinist named Pettit won the award of 500 dollars offered to the successful lock-picker.

Newell was forced to re-think and he concluded that the main problem was to combat the ability to see or feel the relative positions of the tumblers within the lock. After much experiment, the design of lock known as the *Parautoptic* (Greek, meaning 'concealed from view') emerged. Fundamentally, the idea was to remove the actual operating mechanism of the bolt as far from the key as possible and in fact the principle was one of remote control. The first set of levers actuated a second set which, in turn, actuated a third group permitting the bolt to be moved.

Keys to the Parautoptic lock; A: with separate bits aligned; B: with bits rearranged to fit individual lock.

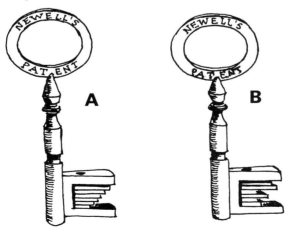

38

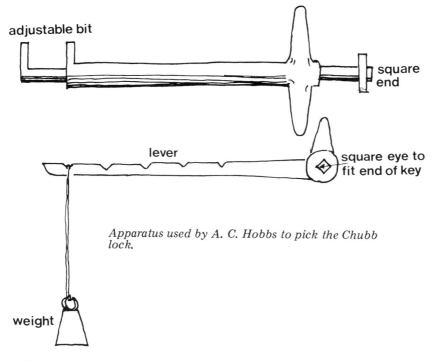

adjustable bit

square end

lever

square eye to fit end of key

Apparatus used by A. C. Hobbs to pick the Chubb lock.

weight

An award of 2,000 dollars was offered to anyone succeeding in picking the Parautoptic lock which in its final form had a key with twelve separate bits, the permutations of arrangements running into many millions. There is no record of this lock ever having been picked. Obviously, the cost of such a mechanism was extremely high and its use was limited to banks and similar premises.

The interest in locks and lock-picking continued unabated and London was the main centre for the lock-picking contests. These culminated in the most startling of all in 1851, the year of the Great Exhibition at Crystal Palace, when a visiting American locksmith called Hobbs caused a major upset. He began his activities in England by calling at the premises of Mr Chubb where he took up the nearest six lever detector lock and quietly picked it open without fuss or bother. Mr Chubb could not accept this and insisted that it was a pure fluke. Hobbs countered this by publicly announcing his intention to repeat the process in public and within a maximum of thirty minutes.

A committee of eleven men, some English, some American, was convened to witness the performance and it duly issued the following statement: 'We, the undersigned, hereby certify that we attended an invitation sent us by A. C. Hobbs of the City of New York, to witness an attempt to open a lock throwing three bolts and having six levers, affixed to the iron door of a strong room built for the depository of valuable papers; and that we severally witnessed the operation which Mr Hobbs commenced at thirty five minutes past eleven o'clock a.m., and opened the lock within 25 minutes. Mr Hobbs, having been requested to lock it again with his instruments, accomplished this in the short space of seven minutes, without the slightest injury to the lock or the door.'

Since this lock had been regarded as impregnable, even by Her Majesty's Government, Chubb's chagrin can be well imagined. He immediately set to work, however, to effect modifications which did, in fact, improve the efficiency of the lever lock.

Hobbs's visit to London was not yet over and he looked round for fresh fields to conquer. The obvious one was the Bramah lock which had rested inviolate in the shop in Piccadilly for fifty years. This was universally accepted as unpickable and in the acceptance of defeat, no pick-lock had made an attempt upon it for many years. Having announced his intentions, the procedure of the committee was repeated, very stringent conditions were laid down and Hobbs was offered thirty days in which to complete his mission. The task took ten days at an average of some four hours per day. The committee and Joseph Bramah were summoned and Hobbs quietly opened the lock. Like Chubb, Bramah was shattered and he insisted that the lock had obviously been damaged. Hobbs, in turn, insisted that the lock be tested with the proper key and when this worked perfectly, the committee ruled that Hobbs be paid the 200 guineas.

Bramah protested against this ruling and a lengthy correspondence ensued, which is reported in full in 'Construction of Locks and Safes' by A. C. Hobbs, but ultimately Bramah capitulated.

The special instruments used by Hobbs are of particular interest and the key which opened the Chubb lock must be one of the most famous in the world although it is hardly in the same category as the masterpiece keys of the previous century. Without entering into a complete description of the action of this apparatus, the basis of the operation was that the weight on the cord maintained a constant pressure on the inside of the lock, and successive adjustments of the key were recorded by the faint movements of the arm, enabling Hobbs to plot the entire internal mechanism. For the Bramah lock, Hobbs adopted another special piece of equipment consisting of a thin steel rod, drilled at one end and having two long projecting teeth, a plain steel needle, another needle rather like a crochet hook and a very thin brass plate on which he recorded all the positions of the eighteen sliders in the lock.

Further challenges followed and the permutations possible with multi-bitted keys became astronomical but the keys of this period were unremarkable and, from the collector's viewpoint, of technical rather than decorative interest. It should be remembered that the new developments of Bramah, Chubb and Day and Newell were all expensive items and did not find their way on to the doors and furniture of the average small house. The warded lock still held sway in this market and continued to do so until well into the twentieth century. Therefore, many large keys with involved bits, Georgian wire bows and some turning on the shank were still produced.

There was, however, one type of key that was unusual, decorative and will make an attractive addition to a key collection. This was the key to the French night latch.

The invention of this latch has, for long, been attributed to an Englishman – Odell – in 1792 and the present author, in previous impressions of this book, has repeated the much publicised statement.

The French night latch was based upon the other type of door-fastening which has been mentioned; that was the lifting latch, which pivoted at one end instead of sliding like the conventional bolt.

The earliest attempts at imparting some degree of security to this lever were by using a latch lifter, these being hook-like or sickle-shaped pieces of iron which have been unearthed from time to time. It has been suggested that these were used as rudimentary turning keys, being inserted through a hole in the door and twisted to move a sliding bolt. It seems more likely that the hook action lifted a latch on the inner face of the door. These lifters are extremely rare and dates are uncertain but the curved specimen which is illustrated overleaf shows sixteenth-century influence.

Donald Dion of Quebec has queried the inconsistency of a *French* latch invented by an Englishman and his research in the 1980s revealed that these spade-like keys, used to lift latches rather than

41

revolve in locks, were mentioned in a French book of 1627. The writer, Mathurin Jousse, believed that this French latch was invented by Franciscan friars and subsequent writers have said that it was used extensively in monasteries. Indeed, the names Cordeliere and Capucine have often been applied to these devices. Since these are both branches of the Franciscan order, M. Jousse was probably correct. This form of latch and key was most widely used by religious orders and the keys became known as *clefs de soeurs*, *clefs de cloitre* or *passe-partout*.

The author suggests that Odell probably *introduced* the French night latch to Britain or perhaps gave his name to a modification of the key, since all the early ones have long stems and the later British versions are abbreviated.

Whilst the latch fell into disuse in France in the early nineteenth century, it enjoyed some popularity in Britain. In Scotland it was used quite extensively and in Edinburgh it became known as the Edinburgh latch; in Glasgow it was placed mainly on outside lavatories and back gates.

Several manufacturers specialised in the supply of French latches and an advertisement from a 1914 catalogue prices them at 23 shillings and 6 pence per dozen! Production in a very small way has continued and the last known order for replacement keys was placed in 1989 with Charles Laing and Sons of Edinburgh by the Cistercian monks of Mount Melleray Abbey in southern Ireland, who had been searching for replacement keys since 1973.

Today in Britain, French night latch keys are very rare and antique dealers who know their history are even rarer! It is, however, occasionally possible to see the typical brass escutcheon plate left on a door. To find one with the latch in working order is very unusual.

At this time, another device on the same principle appeared but the inventor is not known. This was the lift-up night latch. The plain but strange key had a simple solid shank loosely pivoted at the last 20 mm and turning back at right angles to the main stem. The key entered a round hole of some 9 mm diameter, the end was pushed back by a spring and the key was turned to raise the latch. These latches and their keys are less commonly found than the French pattern.

Latches, then, were discarded; wards, although still common, were becoming obsolete; and the eventful period of lockmaking

Night latch and latch keys

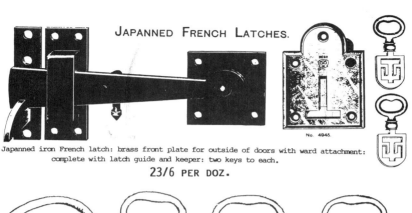

JAPANNED FRENCH LATCHES.

No. 4945.

Japanned iron French latch: brass front plate for outside of doors with ward attachment: complete with latch guide and keeper: two keys to each.

23/6 PER DOZ.

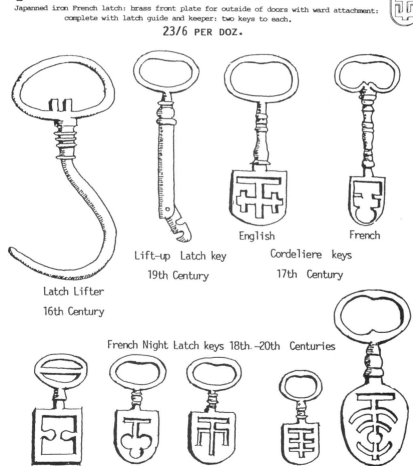

Latch Lifter
16th Century

Lift–up Latch key
19th Century

English

Cordeliere keys
17th Century

French

French Night Latch keys 18th.–20th Centuries

43

which began with Barron in 1778 terminated with Yale in the 1860s.

Linus Yale was a leading bank lock manufacturer who in 1844 patented a lock which was quite different from the usual type produced in his business. This was the cylinder type, owing something to Bramah and something to the ancient Egyptian lock. It is surprising that this lock did not receive any attention at the Great Exhibition of 1851 and it was not until Yale's son, Linus Yale Junior, entered the business and improved and perfected his father's work that the lock made any real impact.

Yale (Jr.) had started a career as a portrait painter and did not develop any mechanical talents until later in life; but his influence, although it does not appear to have attracted the publicity of the protagonists of the Great Lock Controversy, was the most far-reaching of all the great names that preceded him.

The same remark applies here to the Yale cylinder lock as that made in respect of the Bramah lock. To the keen collector, there is no substitute for the real thing and in order really to appreciate the action and quality of any lock, examples can easily be obtained and stripped down.

In Yale and Towne's own words, the astonishing features of the lock at the time of its invention were: 1. its security; 2. master-key possibilities; 3. adaptability; and 4. smallness of key. These features are still important today but the outstanding contribution to lock design made by the pin tumbler cylinder lock was the fact that for the first time a high degree of security was available at comparatively low cost. As has been stated, the top quality locks which have been described were highly costly items of individual hand manufacture. The cylinder lock on the other hand was capable of being mass-produced, as it is today.

From left to right: two keys of the twelfth century, a thirteenth-century key, two of the fourteenth century, one of the fifteenth, and a more modern Barron key.

44

The trade and the collector

As is true for so many industries, one main centre develops over the years which specialises in one particular trade or craft. The centre for locks has, since the times of Elizabeth I, been Willenhall in Staffordshire, and writing of this area in 1732 the Portuguese traveller, Don Manuel Gonzales, said:

'The chief manufacturers of this town are locksmiths, who are reckoned the most expert of that trade in England. They are so curious in this art, that they can contrive a lock so that if a servant be sent into the closet with the master key, or their own, it will show how many times that servant hath gone in at any distance of time, and how many times the lock has been shot for a whole year; some of them being made to discover five hundred or a thousand times. We are informed also that a very fine lock was made in this Town, sold for £20, which had a set of chimes in it that would go at any hour the owner should think fit.'

In 1750 a Dr Richard Wilkes of Willenhall recorded that Willenhall consisted of 'one long street, newly paved, with many good houses' and also that 'more locks of all kinds are made here than in any other town of the same size in England or Europe.' In 1770 there were apparently some 148 lockmakers in the town, but a survey by a Mr Horne in 1841 revealed that there were 268 locksmiths, 76 key-makers, 14 bolt-makers and 13 latch-makers.

In the Post Office Directory of the 1840s the lockmakers are further sub-divided as 'Rim lock makers', 'Trunk lock makers', 'Cabinet lock makers', 'Mortice lock makers', etc. But what is more intriguing is the combination of occupations that some of the smaller manufacturers practised; among those listed by the directory are: 'key stamper and beer retailer', 'door lock maker and beer retailer', 'grocer and trunk lock maker', 'malt shovel tavern keeper and rim lock maker', 'lock maker and provision dealer', 'grocer and key maker', 'cabinet lock maker and

45

Eighteenth-century German rim lock and key. It has two independent spring bolts withdrawn simultaneously from the outside by the pipe key, but there is no means of opening the lock from the inside.

Woolpack tavern', 'key stamper and registrar of births', 'Hope and Anchor and cabinet lock maker', 'auctioneer and locksmith', and 'rim lock and varnish maker'.

The small makers were family affairs with virtually every member contributing, hence the bizarre mixture of trades that was to be found. Not more than half-a-dozen of the above list were of any size, and the remainder were made up of 'small masters' with an average of two apprentices. Mr Horne records that there were at least a thousand boys employed at lock and key-making in the town, even from the age of seven upwards, it being necessary for the youngest to stand on wooden blocks in order to reach the vice. It was an established fact that where so many of the men had been engaged at this work from early childhood they had developed a distortion of their limbs which was a characteristic of the district. The right shoulder blade became displaced and projects, the right leg bends inwards at the knee and the right hand usually is distorted. Even to this day, the district is styled 'Humpshire' by many of the older locals. It has been said that everything the right hand holds takes the position of the file: 'If the poor man carries a limp lettuce or a limp mackerel from Wolverhampton Market, they are never dangled, but held like the file. If he carry nothing, his right hand is in just the same position.'

Much of the work was carried out on a piece-work basis and hours were erratic. Some worked from four or five in the morning until twelve at night, others came and went as they wished, spreading the work over a total working day of some sixteen hours. The beginning of the week often saw much idleness but this was compensated for by eighteen-hour days at the end of the week. They often took their meals at the vice: 'You see a locksmith and his two apprentices, with a plate before each of them, heaped up (at the best of times, when they can get such things) with potatoes and lumps of something or other, but seldom meat, and a large slice of bread in one hand; your attention is called off for a few minutes and on turning round again, you see the man and boys filing at the vice.'

The essential processes of manufacture of locks and keys at this time in the nineteenth century were forging, which consisted of the traditional blacksmith's work with fire and bellows and hammering into approximate shape, and pressing, by means of presses of various sizes. The press consisted of a heavy vertical screw surmounted by a horizontal lever which carried a heavy weight at one end. One of the lever arms is spun round with a jerk, causing the screw to turn sharply and descend with the die or

Eighteenth- and nineteenth-century keys. A: safe key; B: pipe key with spring 'stopper' (dirt excluder); C, D: French keys, typical of Continental practice.

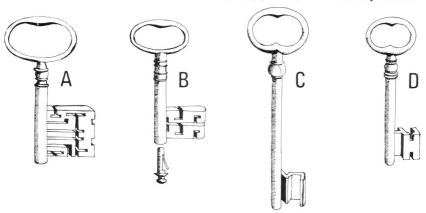

cutter that is attached to it, thereby trimming the metal placed underneath to the required shape.

A similar process was used for keys, namely stamping, which was effected by placing the end of a red hot rod of iron straight from the forge into a half mould of the key, formed in a solid block or anvil. A heavy weight was then raised between vertical guides by means of a cord, the weight having formed on its underside the other half of the key mould. When the cord was released, the weight fell suddenly and the two halves of the mould met, moulding the rough shape of the key and trimming off the surplus metal around it simultaneously. The solid metal which, at this stage, filled the ring or bow, was also pressed out in the same way. The next stage for pipe keys was piercing which consisted of drilling with a treadle-operated machine like a lathe. The final process was the one of filing; the whole key was finished and made bright, the bow received its final shaping and the clefts for the wards cut both by file and cold chisel.

The apprenticeship system was practised extensively in the nineteenth century and the small masters took apprentices at any age at which they could work. Some of them used apprentices only, and so saved the cost of paying wages to the intermediate grade of 'journeyman'. These masters took on new apprentices as soon as those working for them finished their agreed period of time. The boys mostly came from other towns bringing with them an extra suit of clothes and a small apprenticeship fee. The masters then were responsible for providing them with food, lodging and clothing during the time of their contract.

The result of this system was that, on completing his apprenticeship, the now qualified journeyman found it almost impossible to obtain employment as such and was forced to become a small master himself and take on apprentices as his master did. This accounted for the fact that, at that time in the 1840s, there were very few manufacturers of any size and an increasing number of small masters and apprentices.

The Willenhall makers looked mainly to Wolverhampton for a market for their products, and it was common practice for the master and an apprentice or two to trudge off to the dealer or factory in Wolverhampton on a Saturday, loaded with the results of their week's work, spending part of their earnings in the Wolverhampton market before returning home. It was said at the time that nowhere else in the country could compete with Willenhall for cheap locks and that the men worked hard for very

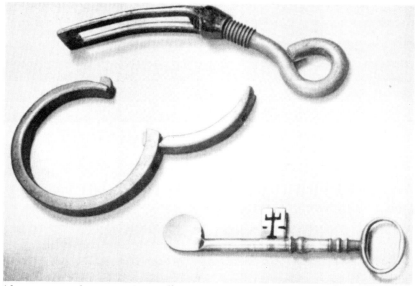

Above, top and centre: ring padlock, made in England c. 1850, and key. The key compresses the ring to release the hook which locks the hinged section of the iron ring.
Above, bottom: key with a bow at each end. This key would pass right through the lock and could be turned from both sides, for example to enable a prisoner clandestinely to absent himself from his cell or to prevent a cleaner from being accidentally locked in a prison cell.

poor reward, and yet their loyalty to the town was strong. Horne quoted an example of this:

'Some years ago, a factor who had projected a Manufactory in Brussels, engaged some five and twenty Willenhall men, whom he was at the expense of taking over. He gave them all work, and from hard earned wages of nine to fifteen shillings a week, these 'practised' hands found themselves able to earn £3 a week and upwards. But they were not satisfied and began to feel uncomfortable; first, one left and returned home; then another; then one or two; till in the course of a few weeks, every man had returned to Willenhall — there to work harder and earn less.'

The craft method, which differed little from medieval practice, continued for many years, although much progress was being made in the establishment of factories and the use of machinery in America. Even from the London factory of Hobbs and Co. A. C. Hobbs reports:

'A number of machines, worked by steam power, are employed in shaping the several pieces of metal contained in a lock; and all the several pieces are deposited in labelled compartments, one to each kind of piece. The machines are employed — in some cases to do coarse work, which they can accomplish more quickly than it can be done by men; and in other cases to do delicate work which they can accomplish more accurately than men; but so far is this converting the men into lowly paid automatons (as some might suppose), that the manufacturers are better able to pay good wages for the handicraft labour necessary in putting the locks together than for forming the separate parts by hand; just as the 'watchmaker' as he is called, who puts the separate parts of the watch together, is a better paid mechanic than the man who is engaged in fabricating any particular parts of the watch.'

Although Willenhall remains the leading centre for locks the position today is vastly different from that of the 1840 era. Lockmakers and allied manufacturers are listed in the Yellow Pages of the telephone directory, but the greatest survivor from the early Victorian period is Josiah Parkes and Sons Ltd. Beginning as iron merchants in 1840, Josiah and his brother William merchanted a great variety of goods, from mole traps to clothes horses, from ash pans to carpenters' tool baskets and, of course, locks and keys. In later years, the company turned to manufacturing locks and by 1906 had risen well above the 'small master and two apprentices' standard and then employed the considerable number of thirty-five employees. By 1913 the number engaged had swollen to one hundred and in the 1970s it is well over 1,800 and is the dominant company in the town having merged with the Chubb Group in 1965.

Undoubtedly the best display of locks and keys as far as the comprehensive coverage from Ancient Egyptian to modern magnetic locks is that in the Science Museum in London.

The metal used for the manufacture of keys continued to be iron for much of the nineteenth century, for although mild steel evolved around 1740 its use was confined mainly to rolled strip and did not gain wider application until later Victorian times. Steel had also been employed in key-making for some time, and many 'masterpiece' keys are said to be of 'forged steel'. The terms often cause confusion and a brief explanation may be helpful.

Iron is the basic metal obtained by heating the special type of rock that contains iron ore and in ancient and medieval times a charcoal furnace was used to attain the intense heat required to smelt the metal from the rock. Ironworks were therefore sited where a plentiful supply of timber was readily available, and this accounted for much of the destruction of the forests of England in the Middle Ages. The resultant material from the furnace still contained a great deal of slag or impurities and this was eliminated by constant hammering. It was discovered that varying amounts of hammering, re-heating and quenching produced different properties and degrees of hardness, and the type which evolved for swords, daggers and knives became known as steel, although its exact properties could not be evaluated as they are for various grades of the metal today. The essential difference between iron and steel lies in the carbon content, which in wrought iron is less than 0·2 per cent, but may be up to 5 per cent in steel. Steel also contains small quantities of other elements.

Returning to our subject of keys, it is not easy to distinguish between iron and steel, the colour is much the same, although the keen eye may be able to detect a rather more silver-white look to the iron. Experienced workmen can often differentiate by the musical note emitted when the metals are struck but a more certain test is to dab the sample lightly with dilute nitric or sulphuric acid. The iron surface will remain unaltered, or only a minute stain will appear, the steel, however, due to the liberation of carbon will show a black mark. A powerful magnifying glass will also show the presence of slag in the iron but not in the steel.

Until 1870 iron was obtainable either wrought (from which keys were made as previously described) or cast; the latter having a higher carbon content and being hard and brittle, was unsuited to key manufacture. A later innovation was the process of malleable casting which incorporated an annealing method to free the iron from nearly all of its carbon, thereby producing an iron with virtually the same qualities as the traditional wrought variety.

Malleable casting of keys was adopted to some extent and was found particularly useful for the cheap standardised locks with simple wards and with possibly as few as six variations on the ward arrangement. For these keys, the protracted processes of stamping, pressing and filing could be eliminated and hand labour reduced to the finishing or fettling operation. Similar sand-casting methods had, of course, been used for some time in the lock trade for the production of solid wards in brass.

Occasionally an unfettled cast key may be found, which can puzzle the key collector as, having the nose of the bit solid, it would seem to be made for a lock with a spring bolt (which would make it of some antiquity) and yet the cuts for the wards appear to be typically late Victorian. The explanation of this is that malleable cast keys invariably had the nose of the bit continuous in order to prevent breakage during casting. The small nib was removed in the fettling as also were other evidences of the casting, such as the 'flash', or small line formed at the junction of the two halves of the mould and any roughness in the clefts of the bit. Another indication of a cast key can be the manner in which the cuts of the bit are tapered outwards from the centre, so that the sand comes cleanly away from the pattern. Malleable cast keys are still produced in small quantities and are mostly available in the form of blanks from which replacement keys for old locks can be cut with saw and file. One Willenhall foundry still produces blanks from very old patterns for church door locks and even one for a typical jail lock — the key being some ten inches in length and weighing almost two pounds.

A wood stock lock made in Scotland in the eighteenth century, with ornamental brass fittings and a keyhole escutcheon fixed to the wood. It has been much restored but the forend and rose of the knob are missing.

Malleable cast keys

Although ferrous metals have always been the most commonly used materials for the making of keys, occasional examples of brass or bronze may be found. Some of these may have been made for an opening ceremony or special purpose, while others, like Admiralty keys, were specifically made in this spark-free alloy to obviate the possibility of explosions in powder magazines.

Ceremonial keys of silver, usually in plush lined cases, sometimes crop up in antique shops. These are invariably attractive, but non-functional, being made for purely decorative purposes and not to fit any lock.

A group of typical standardised keys to Victorian door locks, and (right) a key 'blank' for cutting by a blacksmith.

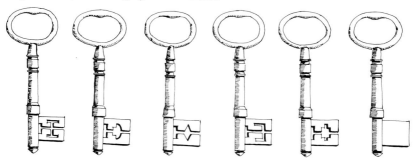

It is clearly impossible to show in any book the seemingly infinite variety of bow shapes, bit patterns, and stem designs that may be encountered in the realm of keys, but it is hoped that the collector will at least, in this small work, gain some basic guidance. As in any other form of collecting, the greatest satisfaction is to be gained from the search in obscure places — the lucky find at negligible cost and the restoration of what is regarded as scrap into a sparkling specimen of the old keymakers' art.

Probably the nineteenth century will provide the biggest proportion of the average collection — the earlier part of that period still continuing, in the main, with the traditional warded-lock keys in the Georgian manner and the latter part of the century reflecting the transition to contemporary locks and keys. The former will be prized for their hand craftsmanship and the latter more for the technical implications. The acquisition of masterpiece keys (such as can be envied at the Victoria and Albert

A powder magazine lock, of uncertain date. Lock and key are made wholly of brass, to eliminate the risk of a spark. It does not have a through keyhole, but a draw-back handle enables anyone shut inside to get out.

Museum) is hardly likely; these very rarely come on to the open market and should they do so, the cost for the best examples could reach four or even five figures.

Nevertheless, this is no deterrent, for interesting collections can be formed by the expenditure of time and initiative rather than money, and in view of the extreme scarcity of the exhibition type of specimen, the possessor of a deep purse enjoys no great advantage in this field of collecting.

The most obvious but least fruitful source from which to start a collection is the antique shop. It is true that some shops do have keys from time to time but they are few and far between and, of course, prices are high. The reader who decides to try his hand at this sort of collection as a change from the more common forms is recommended to visit the older type of ironmongers' shop, usually found in the smaller country towns. The request for 'Any keys?' will invariably provoke the counter question: 'To fit what lock?' The reply that just any old keys will be of interest is usually greeted with some incredulity, but more often than not an old wooden box is unearthed containing a motley selection of keys of all shapes and sizes. Admittedly most of these will be of little value to the collector but among them are often found good specimens which the shopkeeper will sell for 'A bob each?'

Locksmiths are, of course, rather more knowledgeable on values but as they occasionally find their box of 'spares' useful for replacement keys to old locks they are sometimes reluctant to part with them. However, they are worth visiting although any purchase made will probably be at fairly high cost, as the locksmith will base his price, not on any rarity or antique footing but on the fact that a new blank of the same size will cost him a pound or two (or even more for the really large keys).

Builder's yards and workshops often have collections of rusty, dirt-encrusted items; others may be hidden under a plumber's bench or discovered lying in the corner of the 'chippie's' shop from which many a little treasure can emerge. Junk shops are another obvious hunting ground, as are the boxes of miscellanea at auctions. A watchful eye should be kept on old property scheduled for demolition — worm-infested old doors can often be diverted from the site bonfire long enough to unscrew the lock and acquire the key to fit it. Perhaps the best source of all,

A eighteenth-century German rim lock of usual action, with a lift-up bolt operated by pressing down the lever handle on either side and two bevelled sliding spring bolts which are withdrawn by the key only from either side.

although rapidly diminishing in number, is the old traditional local blacksmith and a browse around some really old premises can reveal a treasure trove of rusty iron, some of which, with loving treatment, can be converted into a gem of the collection.

Perhaps the most surprising aspect of key collecting is the almost total ignorance prevailing everywhere on the subject; few locksmiths (whilst all are well versed in the practice of cutting modern Yale and Chubb keys) have any knowledge of the history of their craft. No doubt antique dealers with some knowledge of antique keys do exist, but so far the author has failed to meet one; all, without exception, have, for example, been fascinated yet mystified by the French night latch key carried on his key-ring.

One dealer was reluctant to accept the fact that the key he was offering for £5 was not that of a seventeenth-century strong box (as he had been assured) but quite a common mid-Victorian door key. Many padlock keys of the past hundred years have fairly elaborate bows, the trefoil and quatrefoil designs of the Middle Ages having been revived; when some of these have gathered a good quota of rust and pitting a markedly antique appearance is formed. Whilst these need not be despised, since a collection of them is still attractive and worthwhile, obviously prices should not exceed a few pence each.

Another feature which is sometimes regarded as indicative of considerable age is the 'wirebow'. It is true that this type of bow was virtually standard in Georgian and Regency times but it also continued throughout Victoria's reign and, in fact, was still available in blanks for replacement keys until very recently. The shanks or stems of these later keys have very little turning, unlike the earlier ones, and the cuts in the bit are usually straight cut with the saw, rather than 'radiused' to follow the curve of the ward, as the older originals were. Even these indications are not infallible — good replicas are difficult to distinguish and dealers can be excused for offering, in good faith, keys which are perhaps two hundred years younger than they are thought to be. The absence of literature is the real reason for the lack of knowledge.

The manner in which a collection of keys is presented is a matter of individual taste and imagination. A simple and effective way of showing a collection is to mount the keys on hardboard covered with adhesive felt and frame it with light battens. Attractive groups can be arranged with most types of key and with some kinds, such as the wire bow keys, it is possible to grade them right up from keys some 1½ inches in length through to those of

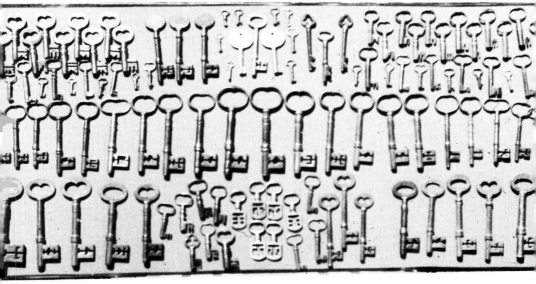

Keys displayed on a board.

10 inches long ($5^1/2$ inches is the size normally regarded as the largest, standardised key of the nineteenth century). The $5^1/2$ inch key is always the one to which the informant refers when telling the collector that 'the key to Mrs Smith's cottage in Church Lane is enormous'! Angler's tales are only equalled by second-hand descriptions of key sizes – as the collector will rapidly discover.

Other methods of displaying keys have been to scatter them apparently haphazardly over stone chimney breasts or to suspend them from the oak beams in an inn, but whatever system is devised, some consideration must be given to the finish to each key.

Most of the newly acquired additions to the collection will be carried home in a rusty state, and restoration can be a somewhat messy but satisfying operation. Unlike coins, no set rules exist, and the ultimate finish can be left to personal preference. Keys which are several hundred years old, however, and are in an

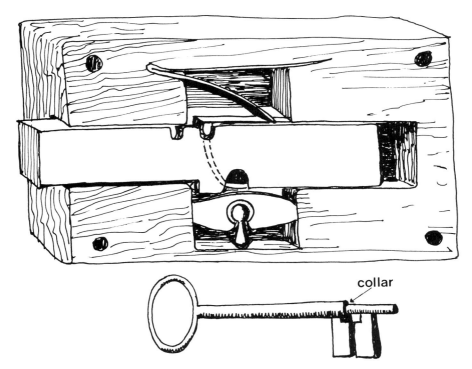

'Banbury' lock and key. Note the collar set part way along the bit — a characteristic of this form of lock. The lock case is of solid oak.

extensively pitted condition are probably most effectively presented by merely removing any superficial scale and not attempting to achieve any great restoration, since this will involve the removal of much of the surface metal in filing down, tending to destroy the original shape. For such time-worn pieces, the traditional look of black corrosion is in any case the most suitable appearance.

Later keys can be fully finished and polished and small needle files are helpful here, for the fine clefts of the bit. Some collectors prefer a 'blue' colour to the steel or iron, and this can be simply achieved by heating in a flame until the blue-black tint is obtained and then quenching in water or oil.

The collection can, of course, be extended to include locks, but unless the more decorative specimens of the sixteenth and

Iron chest lock

A German iron chest lock (seventeenth-century). Pushing the heart-shaped thumb-piece rotates the horizontal shaft, thereby deadlocking the bolts.

seventeenth centuries can be acquired (and this will be both difficult and expensive) the collection will be largely confined to the nineteenth century and be of technical rather than visual interest. There is no reason, however, why a few of the outstanding types of lock should not accompany the key collection — the Bramah has been mentioned and other small brass-cased locks of this period are worth keeping. The occasional Banbury lock can be found in country districts, and with the oak case renovated, these can be pleasant to view and handle. The key, it must be admitted, is the more 'collectable' item, being compact, attractive in itself and doubly so when displayed in groups.

It is often said that many keys have been bought by American tourists and that the supply is now running dry. Certainly, key collecting seems to have captured the imagination of Americans rather more than our own and it is easy to understand that these easily portable pieces, which have attached to them the associations of castles and treasure chests, of oak cottage doors and grim stone jails, have attained some popularity among visitors to this country.

As far as the supply running low, it must be accepted that the discovery of old keys is not so easy as it was, but it must be remembered that many old warded locks and keys are still in daily use in the more remote areas and as demolition or replacement takes place, these can ultimately find their way into your collection.

Thirteenth-century iron key.

60

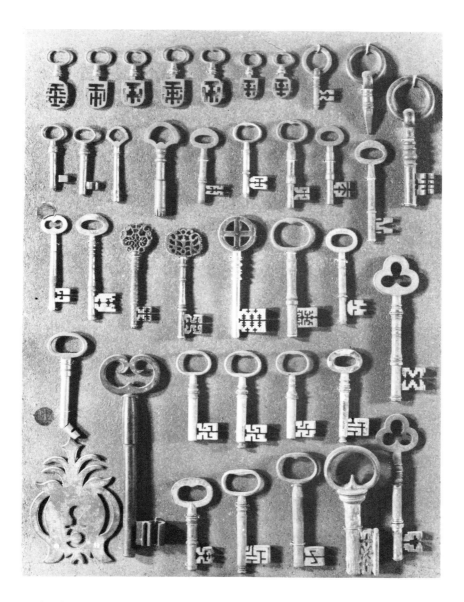

A selection of antique keys in the Company Museum of Josiah Parkes Ltd.

Collection costs

The cost of acquiring objects for any collection is an important factor for the collector. The following notes will provide indications of what one might expect to pay for keys and are based upon actual sums realised during the 1990s.

Considering their antiquity, the cost of Roman, Gallic and medieval keys is surprisingly low. The 1999 price for an undamaged Roman bronze ring key with little corrosion is about £50. Other small keys in this group, including the Gallic type hammered from sheet bronze, can be obtained for as little as £15. Larger medieval keys can reach about £100 each but are often offered in small batches of various sizes, making individual costing difficult.

In the Renaissance period, the key, in addition to its function as an implement of security, became an art form and status symbol. The so-called 'chamberlain keys' were actually staffs of office, many of which had solid, useless bits or no bits at all. The cost of these masterpiece symbols puts them beyond the range of most collectors, who search for specimens of true workaday tools from the past two thousand years. The simpler everyday Renaissance keys can occasionally still be acquired in a heap of miscellaneous items at about £5 each but may attain three-figure sums in the auction houses.

The intricate craftsmanship of the Renaissance is shown in some keys that exceed the purely functional simplicity of an everyday item but do not aspire to masterpiece standard. These are mostly of the Venetian type and have round, oval or triangular bows with frets that are brazed rather than chiselled from the solid iron. Prices for these are between £100 and £200.

Another key of the medieval and Renaissance periods is the 'Banbury' lock key. The design of this typical blacksmith's item has not changed for the past four hundred years or more, and precise dating is impossible. The condition will range from dug-up as a pile of red dust to pristine, retrieved from a warm dry cupboard. These too may be purchased for £5 or so each.

The costs of nineteenth-century keys, which are now antiques, vary mainly by size. The warded type bit, wire bow and turned stem, typical of keys of this period, can be found in 50 mm casket keys at £3 each or 300 mm castle keys from £100. Sizes between these extremes range from £20 to £40. The front-door key of 140-160 mm is the most popular size. Trefoil, quatrefoil and other bow variations often found in the larger church-door keys of 150-200 mm usually reach prices around £30 to £50.

The interesting variations of Victorian padlock keys, which are now quite rare, make these collectable, and they can be found on market stalls at around £2 or £3 each. French night-latch keys were still in production as replacements in 1950 at one shilling (5p) each. Although such items have until recently been discarded as valueless, they are now selling at a virtually standard price of £25 each.

The figures given should be treated with caution when assessing present-day values, and it must be stressed that the prices paid in prestigious salerooms will not be achieved at a local antiques centre; there are still bargains to be found in junk shops and market stalls. Also, past prices are not necessarily subject to increase. At some recent international sales Renaissance keys have achieved prices of around £20 each.

Collectors should beware reproductions. Many types of antique key are not difficult to copy, and in the 1950s there were available many cheap castings of keys, horse brasses and other brassware items. These were unashamedly reproductions and not intended to deceive, but now that they are less common and have acquired some patina of age their identification can be dubious.

Another reproduction is the one-off replacement for an old lock. Many of these are indistinguishable from the seventeenth- and eighteenth-century originals, but again there was no intention to deceive. Because of the length of time needed for pattern-making, casting and fettling, the final cost exceeds the price of the genuine antique. So the problem of fake keys, unlike some other forms of collecting, is not a big one. Happy cagophily.

Comparative sizes of keys

Early keys

Egyptian, 2000 BC (wood)

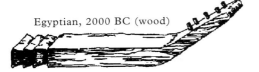

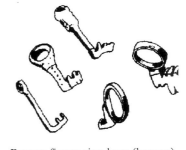

Roman finger-ring keys (bronze)

Early Greek keys (wood)

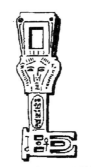

Egyptian, 300 BC

130 mm

Romano-Gallic
sixth century (bronze)

63 mm

55 mm

59 mm

Roman bronze keys

83 mm

Roman iron key; barrel-type lock   125 mm

64

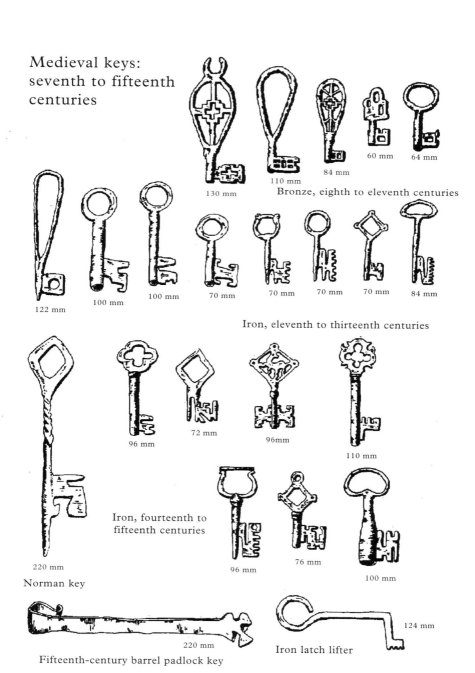

Medieval keys:
seventh to fifteenth
centuries

60 mm

64 mm

84 mm

110 mm

130 mm

Bronze, eighth to eleventh centuries

122 mm

100 mm

100 mm

70 mm

70 mm

70 mm

70 mm

70 mm

84 mm

Iron, eleventh to thirteenth centuries

96 mm

72 mm

96mm

110 mm

Iron, fourteenth to
fifteenth centuries

96 mm

76 mm

100 mm

220 mm

Norman key

220 mm

Fifteenth-century barrel padlock key

124 mm

Iron latch lifter

65

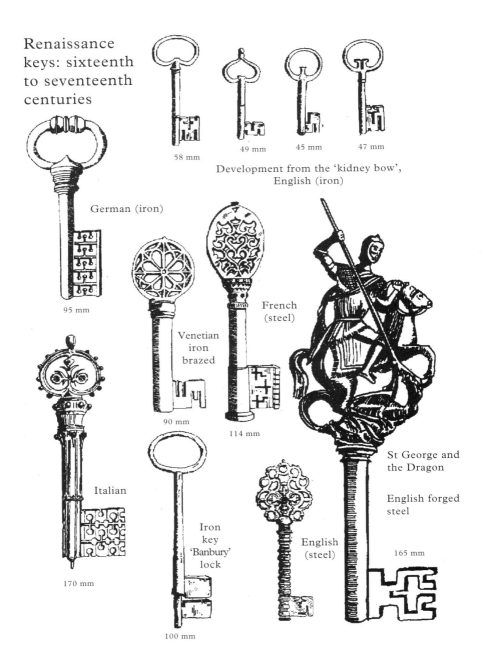

Renaissance
keys: sixteenth
to seventeenth
centuries

49 mm

45 mm

47 mm

58 mm

Development from the 'kidney bow',
English (iron)

German (iron)

95 mm

French
(steel)

Venetian
iron
brazed

90 mm

114 mm

Italian

170 mm

Iron
key
'Banbury'
lock

English
(steel)

St George and
the Dragon

English forged
steel

165 mm

100 mm

66

Classical keys: seventeenth to eighteenth centuries

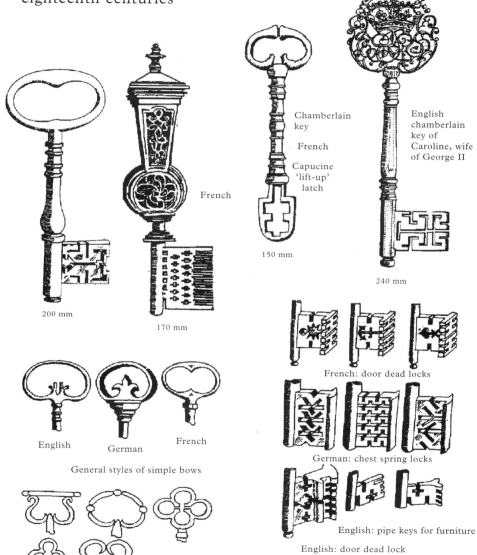

French

Chamberlain key

French

Capucine 'lift-up' latch

150 mm

English chamberlain key of Caroline, wife of George II

240 mm

200 mm

170 mm

English

German

French

General styles of simple bows

Eighteenth-century variations on medieval themes

French: door dead locks

German: chest spring locks

English: pipe keys for furniture

English: door dead lock

General national characteristics of key bits

Industrial keys: eighteenth to nineteenth centuries

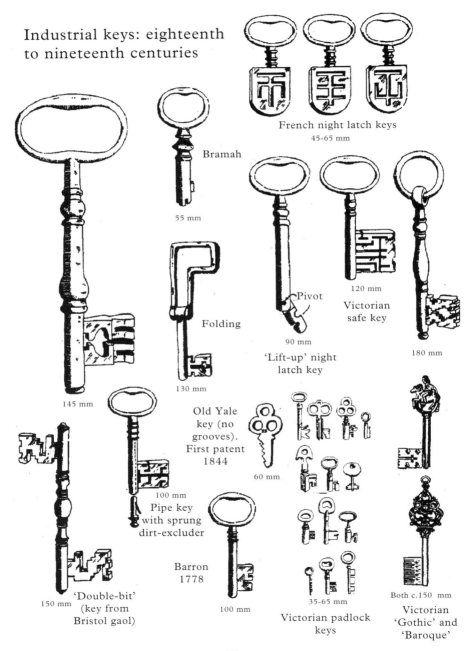

French night latch keys
45-65 mm

Bramah

55 mm

120 mm

Victorian safe key

Folding

Pivot

130 mm

'Lift-up' night
latch key

90 mm

180 mm

145 mm

Old Yale
key (no
grooves).
First patent
1844

60 mm

100 mm

Pipe key
with sprung
dirt-excluder

Barron
1778

'Double-bit'
(key from
Bristol gaol)

150 mm

100 mm

Victorian padlock
keys

35-65 mm

Both c.150 mm

Victorian
'Gothic' and
'Baroque'

Further reading

Butter, J. F. *An Encyclopaedia of Locks and Builders' Hardware*. Josiah Parkes & Sons, Willenhall, 1979. Useful reference work.

Currer-Briggs, N. *Chubb Collectanea*. Chubb & Sons, 1968.

Disraeli, B. *Sybil, or the Two Nations*. 1845; reprinted, Penguin, 1980. Includes a very graphic account of working conditions in the lock and key industry at that date in the fictional town of 'Woodgate' based upon Willenhall.

Eras, V. J. M. *Locks and Keys Throughout the Ages*. Lips & Company, 1957. Probably still the best and most comprehensive publication on the subject.

Evans, J., and Allman, G. *One Hundred Years of Keymaking*. Arthur Hough & Sons Ltd (key manufacturers of Essington, Wolverhampton), 1983. Beautifully produced, with superb line drawings.

Glasson, M. *Willenhall Town Trail*. Walsall Museum and Art Gallery, 1987. Gives a brief history of the town, followed by a guided walk including the main lock-manufacturing area of the town.

Hedges, N., and Beynon, H. *Born to Work*. Pluto Press, 1982. Working life in the West Midlands in photographs and first-hand accounts, much of it based on the experiences of workers at Josiah Parkes's factories in Willenhall.

Phillips, Peter. *Locks and Keys*. Boydell & Brewer Ltd, 1998.

Stewart, D. *Standard Guide to Key Collecting*. Key Collectors International, USA, 1990.

Tildesley, J. C. 'Locks and Lockmaking' in S. Timmins (editor), *Birmingham and the Midland Hardware District*, 1866.

Varndell, G. *A Short History of Lock Making in Willenhall*. Walsall Museum and Art Gallery, 1978.

Places to visit

Birmingham Museum and Art Gallery, Chamberlain Square, Birmingham B3 3HQ. Telephone: 0121 303 2834. Website: www.birmingham.gov.uk/bmag (Fine examples of European workmanship, much of it on a large scale.)

Bantock House, Bantock Park, Finchfield Road, Wolverhampton WV3 9LQ. Telephone: 01902 552195.

J. H. Blakey and Sons (Security) Ltd, Burnley Road Works, Burnley Road, Brierfield, Lancashire BB95 5AD. Telephone: 01282 613593. (This outstanding collection of locks, keys, strongboxes and safes formed by Mr Neville Blakey is open strictly by appointment.)

Blists Hill Open Air Museum, Legges Way, Madeley, Telford, Shropshire TF7 5DU. Telephone: 01952 586063. Website: www.vtel.co.uk/igmt (A locksmith's shop giving demonstrations.)

The Lock Museum, 54-55 New Road, Willenhall, West Midlands WV13 2DA. Telephone: 01902 634542. (A restored locksmith's house and working workshop with a collection covering all aspects of the trade and the people employed in it.)

Science Museum, Exhibition Road, South Kensington, London SW7 2DD. Telephone: 0207 938 8000. Website: www.nmsi.ac.uk (Extensive collections of locks and security mechanisms from ancient Egypt to the present day.)

Treadgold Museum, Bishop Street, Portsmouth, Hampshire PO1 3DA. Telephone: 02392 824745. (Restored premises of ironmonger and steel merchant, with stock of keys and locks still *in situ*.)

Victoria and Albert Museum, Cromwell Road, South Kensington, London SW7 2RL. Telephone: 0207 938 8500. Website: www.vam.ac.uk (Fine examples of intricate workmanship in locks and masterpiece keys.)

York Castle Museum, Eye of York, York YO1 9RY. Telephone: 01904 613161. Website: www.york.gov.uk/heritage/museums/castle (Small collection and display of keys over several centuries.)

The Master Locksmiths Association (Senior Executive, Lorraine Stanley), 5d Great Central Way, Woodford Halse, Daventry, Northamptonshire NN11 3PZ. Telephone: 01327 262255.

Index

St George and the Dragon — a seventeenth-century English forged steel key.